Inside the Mind of a Poet

Inside the Mind of a Poet

A Journey through Life

Cheryl Brandon

Copyright © 2010 by Cheryl Brandon.

Library of Congress Control Number: 2010911179
ISBN: Hardcover   978-1-4535-5912-3
                Softcover   978-1-4535-4793-9
                Ebook   978-1-4535-4794-6

All rights reserved. No part of this book may be reproduced or transmitted in any form or by any means, electronic or mechanical, including photocopying, recording, or by any information storage and retrieval system, without permission in writing from the copyright owner.

This book was printed in the United States of America.

To order additional copies of this book, contact:
Xlibris Corporation
1-888-795-4274
www.Xlibris.com
Orders@Xlibris.com
82152

Dedication

I would like to dedicate this book to Mr. Divine and Maurice Mills.

Contents

Acknowledgments 9
Introduction 11

Chapter One:
In the Soul, There Is God and Love

I Put You First 15
I Said a Poem 16
Love 17
Words Behind the Pen 18
A Mansion 19
A Mind That's Deep 20
Ms. Poetry 22
Another Vow, Same Prayer 23
A Conversation about the Morning 25
Love Letters to a Soldier 27
In His Words 28
Free 29
Teena Marie 30
Beautiful 31
Farewell to Our Father 32
Shadow 34
Just Because 35
Searching, for a Soul 36
A Message from God 37

Chapter Two:
In the Heart and Body, There Is Romance and Seduction

Inside of You, Inside of Me 41
Oh, What a Feelin' 42
We're Still Dancing 44
Flesh against Flesh 45
Cut 47

Passion..48
Oral Conversation..49
The Problem Is 50
A Movie..51
Easy..52
Slippery When Wet..53
Physical Attraction..54
My Daydream..55
Peep Show..56
Men 57

Chapter Three:
In the Mind, There Was Pain and Healing

Protect Me, Lord..61
A Positive Person...62
She Kept Yelling Out 63
Don't Call Him . . . Nigger..65
Three Strikes Were Out...66
Raped 68
Rage...69
Blackout..70
Something in Common.. 71
High, off life...72
Plain Clothes 73
Nothing Like My Mother...74
Home on the Train...76
Affair.. 77
Ladies..78
Someone's Crying for Help 79
Not in the Least 81
Locked 82
What's This World Coming To?..83
Cover Girl...85
These Eyes..86
What Is Poetry?...87
A Poem for God..88

Acknowledgments

God has truly given me a gift; and I hope my poetry will open some minds, heal some hearts, and touch some souls.

I will always give credit to my mother and father, Frank and Sandra Brandon, whom I love and appreciate.

To my sister Terri, what can I say, you continue to inspire me and you are truly a piece of my rock.

To my brothers Rev and Shaun, you guys provide inspiration on different levels, but I love you both the same.

Special thanks to everyone who supported me and inspired me in more ways than one:

Professor Ruth Ruttenberg; George P. Horton; Sister Dorothy; Rev. Scott Marks; Lia Fiol-Matta, Esq.; Nyeesha Bolland, MSW; Jake Feltman; Jean-Homer Lauture; Camilla Nesbitt; Matilda Outlaw; Rosslyn Wuchinich; Lyle Hickman; Rhonda Jackson; Tracy Richardson; Sharon Estwick; Eldin Elezovic; Sharon Green; LaTonya Grier-Best; Desiree Smith-Spriggs; Renea Butler; Catherine Daniels; Delores Boyd; Monica Lawrence; Nancy Smith; Evelyn Ming and Trina Basey.

Introduction

As I began to write this book, I was interrupted by my youngest nephew, Blake. While in deep thought, he's asking me, while typing on my laptop, "Do I know all the words in the *at* family?" When I looked up, he typed at, cat, bat, sat, rat, hat, fat, that, mat, pat, and oat. I decided to keep this as a part of my introduction because, as I was going inside my world of poetry, my nephew took me inside the mind of a five-year-old.

Everyone has a purpose in life. *Inside the Mind of a Poet* is bringing me closer to my purpose. As I exposed some thoughts in my mind, I found out that God wants me to write poetry. This gift is not a mistake, but a tool to relate to humankind. I entered into this journey called life, seeking salvation, love, romance, wisdom, respect, understanding, education, guidance, healing, dignity, and discipline. On this journey of life, I've discovered me.

Have you ever wondered what someone was thinking? What if you could get inside someone's mind? Well, let me take you inside the mind of a poet, because the heart, body, and soul never lied.

Author Cheryl Brandon

Chapter One:
In the Soul, There Is God and Love

I Put You First

I put you first
When I thirst wisdom
I'd grab your word
And read a verse

I put you first
When I am in need
I get on my knees
And you take me to church

I put you first
Because once upon a time
I only called your name
When I was hurt

I put you first
Because I discovered love
And I love the fact
That you loved me first

You put me first
When you gave me life
And you died for my sins
So I can begin again

You gave me a gift
So I put you first
Even if
I'm the last to get in

I Said a Poem

I said a poem, and someone in the audience blew me a kiss
And nothing can stop me now because God wants me to do this

I said a poem, and the cheers from the audience made me feel proud
I let them inside of my mind and clearly connected with the crowd

I said a poem, because someone has to speak up and talk about it
I said a poem, so you can hear it and won't have to read about it

I said a poem, because I enjoy talking, especially when it's about love
I said a poem, so the world can see what a poet's thinking of

I said a poem, because it helps me express all the things I feel
Come inside the mind of a poet and listen to what we reveal

I said a poem, wishing I can help someone face their truth
Someone once told me, my poems help them
And that's all I need as proof

I said a poem, because once upon a time, that girl in that poem was me
Someone had to tell me, my poem helped them
for me to realize my poems helps me

I said a poem
Hoping my words can inspire someone to be all that they can be

I said a poem to someone
Because someone said a poem to me

Love

Love
A reflection of God
But an image of you
And you look like a star
Your smile shines
And it encourages me to smile
Who are you?
You are God's child
Thank you, Lord
Your son obeys you
You came into his heart
He is your son
And he praises you
Although he speaks to me
I know
He speaks to me through you
Did he tell you I'm changing, Lord?
Look at me
I'm changing for you
You are so amazing
The way you introduced me
To your friend
I thank you
For the blessings, Lord
You've blessed me
Over and over again
I love you, Lord
Because I finally understand
What true love really means
You are my number one Love
Because you are
The true man of my dreams

Words Behind the Pen

My words behind the pen
As I speak to you through pages
Over and over again
My life through different stages

My happiness expressed through love
My sadness expressed through pain
My words behind the pen
As I express my joys and pains

Through these lines I bare my soul
So intimately, I feel naked
Through this pen my stories told
I'll speak the truth if you can take it

My words behind the pen
Can you read between the lines?
I am the one with the pen
And behind this pen
These words are mine

A Mansion

My house may not look like yours
But I'm waiting to move in a mansion
So what, you have marble floors
I'd rather have Christ
Than a house of fashion
From where I'm standing
It doesn't look like a home
Tell me, does God live in your house?
You see, the devil doesn't look in my window
Because God's here
And he's always looking out
One day, I'll be living in a mansion
All white, with white pearly gates
You too can live in God's home
Because God says that it's never too late
I don't mind waiting on my new home
Because this mansion is worth the wait
When God's ready
He will invite me to his home
The address is heaven's gate

A Mind That's Deep

Inside a mind that's deep
Imagine if you can get inside someone's mind
I wonder what people think about?
Is your mind as deep as mine?

I'm deep
Because I'm still thinking when I'm asleep
These are some thoughts in my mind
Come in and take a peek

I often wonder, what was God thinking?
When he created a woman and a man
How did he know to put a heart in a woman?
How did he know to put strength in a man?

I wonder, what my mother was thinking
The day she laid eyes on my dad
Did she know he would be her husband?
Or did my father have to keep coming back?

What if I would've changed my mind at the altar?
Would I have lost the man of my dreams?
Or is the man of my dreams still out there?
And he bypassed me because I'm wearing a ring

What if Barack didn't win the election?
Would we still believe in democracy?
Would we go out and vote again in the future?
Can the government take my vote from me?

Inside a mind that's deep
Come inside, and see what you'll find
Come inside the mind of a poet
Is your mind as deep as mine?

Ms. Poetry

This is my vice
I love to write
I recite lyrics in my sleep
I get deep when I write
Soul searching
When I search for my soul
I unite
My heart, mind, and body
Take off like a flight
I am Ms. America
Red, white, and blue stripes
Salute me, it suits me
These lyrics stems from the root of me
They call me Ms. Poetry
So please introduce me
But I wonder what you see
Do you see? What I see?
I give back through poetry
Because God gave poetry to me

Another Vow, Same Prayer

Do you take this man?
To be your lawful wedded husband
I took those vows
Lord, can I take them again?
We can't start from the end
If we didn't start from the beginning
Let's go back and make it right
And put all the ingredients in it
I want to stand in the kitchen
With obedience in it
Put God at the head of the table
To keep us from sinning
We can get to the middle
If we create a new beginning
I thought I knew it all
I didn't think the devil would get in
Oh, Lord, hear my prayer
I should have trusted you from the beginning
Forgive us for our sins
And the part that I played in it
Because now, I'm on my knees
And my heart is all in it
With unconditional love
And love has no limit

Let's be soul mates forever
Not soul mates for a minute
When I got on my knees
My whole spirit repented
Remake my soul
You made a mate for my soul
Whether death do us part
Whether silver or gold
Let me take my vows again
So I can be at peace with my soul

A Conversation about the Morning

Morning Fresh . . .
The beginning of me is in the morning
A sign of new life stretching and yawning
Awaking my brain without warning
Letting the crack of dawn in
Oh, how I love a brand-new day
The smell of morning is like fresh air
And I believe, it's a message from God
That he still wants me here
Oh, how I love life
And mornings are the best
It's breakfast in bed, its birds singing
New life is morning fresh

Morning Blues . . .
Mornings and I don't mix
I hate getting up in the morning
I hate waking up from a good dream
And compared to nights
Mornings are boring
I like when it's dark outside
You can see the beautiful bright lights
In the morning, you can't go out and party
So you can't compare mornings to nights
Oh, how I love life, in the nighttime
Because I can put on my dancing shoes
At night, I'm singing sweet love songs
In the mornings, I'm singing the blues

Morning Fresh . . .
Keep this in mind morning blues
You can't compare nights to days
Because at night we get on our knees
And ask God, to wake us up to a new day

Love Letters to a Soldier

I love a man in a uniform
You wear your suit with dignity
You put your hat on, like a real man
You dress up when you protect me

You show your strength
With your ribbons and metals
You show your strength
When you lift up our country
The U. S. is a heavy metal
And you're doing all this fighting for me

Wow, how do you do that?
Our country calls, and you're ready to bat
I wonder where the red, white, and blues are at?
And do they really salute?
And take off their hats

I love a man that will die for me
My dear soldier, my heart beats for you
And you don't have to put on a uniform for me
Because I'm in love with the soldier in you

In His Words

In the twenty-two years that I've known her
I've never met her
It was just yesterday
I saw her for the first time
Although she never told me her name
It was her smile that said it all
I was happy to make her acquaintance
In fact, she's the reason you've discovered me
She's the reason my covers blown
So here I am, with my knees on the ground
Because you are the only one
I look up to
And for the first time
I'm at a lost for words
Realizing now, that I never knew it all
And I realize now
That you made her just for me
So I'm realizing that I do have it all
I know it's late, God, but I never thanked you
You were the one
Who introduced me to my wife
And I know now
That I can love her forever
Because I have you
For the rest of my life

Free

My laughs are genuine
My concerns are sincere
Sometimes I cry when I'm happy
And when I'm sad, I shed a tear

I am so full of inspiration
And I love when someone inspires me
I love, with no hesitation
I love myself because I'm free

I love to smile and make jokes
And I don't mind if the joke is on me
What can I say, I am who I am
And I can be who I am
Because I'm free

Teena Marie

These notes create lyrical flows with my pen
Especially when you get high
I jump up and down
And move my feet
Like a tap dancer
With a pair of new shoes
I love your funk
I love your jazz
I love your rhythm
I love your blues
But we've been hitting high notes
Since we were slaves
That's not nothing new
But you see
What these notes make me do
As your voice changes
My pen starts to dance
I create romance
With just the stroke of my pen
Bring that tap dancer back
And hit that high note again
I write about sweet melodies
And three-part harmonies
Ooh, la, la, la
You've inspired me

Beautiful

Beauty is in the eyes of the beholder
So compare it to the stars gleaming
Clusters like diamonds, in my wedding ring
I am like the stars, because you make me glow

When you hold me
I melt like cotton candy in your mouth
I'm sweet, because you're sweet on me
And when you're holding me
I know you see my beauty
That's why I can bare my soul to you

I love that you see the inner me
It's what's inside that makes me unique
And you know, you can have all ten of me
I'll show you when others have to peek

Your compliments touch my heart
Your words sound like music to my ears
You've proved I was beautiful to you
Because you've called me beautiful for years

Although I know I'm beautiful
It's important to me, you know it too
Because your looks don't make you beautiful
It's what's inside of you

Farewell to Our Father

Our father
Was a great man
A strong man
With a giant heart
They say, a small baby makes a big man
He left here 6'8
But came here in a shoe box

My father worked hard all his life
He was loved by his family
He was loved by his wife
And if I had to choose a father again
I'd pray the Lord bring that same man in my life

He was a deacon
Active in his community
And if you messed up
He would put you in your place
He was strong
And kept things together
A great man
That will never be replaced

He was loved by many
He was a giving man
And if he gave his word
Believe me, it was done
My father, born ready to fight
I feel honored that I am your son

But my father decided to go home
His new address is heaven's gate
He knew the Lord was calling him
To come home
But he disobeyed him
And decided to wait

He said, son, what took you so long?
I waited for you
Now I must go
Read some scriptures
To comfort your heart
And repeat my last words
So everyone could know

My brothers were there by his side
And at times, I wasn't around
I love my brothers for being by his side
I'm proud of them for always holding it down

And to my mother
And my sister
I'll always be there for you
I know that God is watching over us
Because I put God in everything that I do

And I'm just thankful
That I made it back home
God's plan was to get me back here
So, Dad, go enjoy your new home
And I'll see you when I get there

In loving memory of Mr. Hunter

Shadow

Do you see the shadow on the wall?
It doesn't look like me
Because it's not me at all
It's someone who wants to be like me
Walks like me, talks like me
But no one gets into my mind
Because no one thinks like me
My 3.7 got me my degree
So step out my shadow
Because you can't follow me
And you can't see
What I can see
I put on glasses
So I can see clearly
Yes wise eyes, multiples
I see rain and sunny skies
I thank God for four eyes
And you don't wear glasses
So stop telling yourself lies
You could never be me
So here's something you should know
You could never shadow me
Because I see myself
Wherever I go

Just Because

He brought me a dozen roses
Just because it's Tuesday
I love him
Because he loves to make me smile
On Wednesday nights
We pray together
God willing, we'll be together
Lord knows I love him
Because I'm praying to have his child
Thursday nights is our date night
But we spend most of our nights making love
On Fridays I reminisce
On how he's keeping me in love
Saturday nights, I give him space
Because he likes to watch the game
On Sundays he cooks my favorite foods
At the table, he's saying the grace
And just because it's Monday
I wrote this poem for you
It doesn't have to be Valentine's Day
It's just because . . .
I love you

Searching, for a Soul

I'm driving down this road called love
And love certainly takes it's toll
How much will it cost to cross that bridge?
Because, I'm searching for a soul

I've traveled from state to state
And this road is very long
How many miles before I get there?
And when I get there, will our souls be gone?

Tell me, do we search for something sweeter
Other than us making love in the cold
Are you only thinking of her body, when you meet her?
Or, are you looking for someone to hold?

You can get to someone's mind if they're weak
But wouldn't you want someone with a mind of their own?
I believe, love is something you keep
That's why, love should be deep in the soul

Although it's not easy to give your heart
And who we love, we can't control
I want someone I can keep in my heart
That's why; I'm searching for a soul

A Message from God

I get the message, Lord
She is no better than he
Although you sent a message through him
You're sending that message to me
Forgive me, Lord
Because he was so dedicated to thee
I interrupted his teaching, Lord
And now he's teaching
Your words to me
I was lost, Lord
We made love
And that's when I lost control
But that wasn't our only connection, Lord
We connected to you through our souls
I know it's wrong, and God
I need you to help me with this one
Please forgive your daughter, Lord
And please have mercy on your son
And yes, I'm speaking for both of us
Because it's you, God, we both trust
Although you sent a message to one of us
You sent that message
So you can hear from both of us

Chapter Two:
In the Heart and Body, There Is Romance and Seduction

Inside of You, Inside of Me

Look deep, look deep inside
And you will discover me
Invite me, inside of you
So you can come inside of me

I want to get closer to you
Introduce me to your intimacy
Let me inside of you
So I can let you inside of me

I want to share your mind
So no one can tell us apart
Inside of you, inside of me
Come inside and look at my heart

I want to explore every inch of your body
Down to every body part
But it's your soul I'm searching for
Because I've discovered that place in your heart

So look deep, look deep
With you is where I want to be
Inside of you
You, inside of me

Oh, What a Feelin'

This joint is jumping
I hear music
So I jump to the ceiling
My heart is pumping
Bump, bump, bump, bump
Oh, what a feeling
Stop for a minute
Let me catch my breath
But I'll keep doing this dance
To the right
If you'll keep playing that music
To the left
That's it, that's it right there
I bet you didn't know
That was my song
Oh, what a feeling
What a feeling it is
To hear you play it
All night long
I love those instruments
The way you play them
Seems as if you never skip a beat
No wonder
I'm jumping to the ceiling
Because you're knocking me off my feet

I'm on a high
Hypnotized, mesmerized
By your sound
Hey, Mr. DJ
Just play that funky music
And let me dance
Until the curtains come down
Oh, what a feeling
I want to move
Move this body
To the beat of your drum
Someone told me
You were playing music over here
Soon as I heard that!
I wanted to come

We're Still Dancing

The music stopped
And yet we're still dancing
We sent the DJ home last night
After we got our last dance in

Everyone's left the party
But we're still out on the dance floor
If the DJ stopped playing the music
What are we dancing for?

Do we hear some music inside?
That no one else seems to hear
Tell the DJ to play another love song
Because we're still dancing in here

Last night the music stopped playing
But something keeps us coming back for more
Last night, we said it was over
But look at us
We're still on the dance floor

So let the DJ come back and play a song
It's obvious, we can't leave the floor
And yet we said it was over
But we still want to dance some more

Flesh against Flesh

As we lay parallel
Flesh against flesh
Stuck to you like glue
My breast on your chest

Slow grind
Your flesh against mine
Feeling the body movement
I get lost in time

Electric heat
Because I feel it inside
Sending shock waves
Up and down my spine

My eyes see this motion
Because I like to keep my eyes open
My lips freeze
I prepare for the explosion

I'm at a loss for words
My hands are moving
Just reaching for what's out there
Your hands are writing music
All through my hair

Pull me closer
As my knees start to shake
Flesh against flesh
To see how much I can take

We're in slow motion
You, me, oil and lotion
My river starts flowing

Your toes separate
They don't want to be together
Some moving up
Some moving down

Up and down my flesh
As I'm against your flesh
I lost this battle
Oh yes, oh yes

Cut

I'm standing there covered in bubbles
The waters pouring down like rain
In my wet birthday suit
Someone's whispering my name

It slipped in when wet
You're behind me so I won't fall
In this scene we're in the shower
But we're not showering at all

The mood is set and the candles are lit
I hear someone singing, lady in red
The lights are dim, I'm ready for action
In this scene, I'm making my way to the bed

I grab the bedpost like a dancer
Because red light special, by TLC, came on
The room is red, and I'm wearing red fishnet
We're about to bring to life, this verse from the song

But then, the music stopped, I heard cut
I was just about to have me some fun
Then the curtains closed, I heard next scene
The director said, this scene is done

Passion

Sipping your passion like wine
I could taste the grapes you stepped in
You're that bottle; you break out at the right time
Aging to perfection

I'm looking to pop you open
Like a cork, I want to get in
But I'd rather you pour it in a glass
So I could be on the outside looking in

Flowing as I tip you over
I say ah, because my mouth is thirsty
The effects of the wine is taking over
I'm tingling inside because you're next to me

What a beautiful feeling to want you
And I love it because it's long and lasting
The wine didn't get me in this mood
It was you, who poured on this passion

Oral Conversation

Speaking in tongues
With no hesitation
I speak to you
You speak to me
We're having an oral conversation
I like to talk
Even though I get tongue tied
You don't say much
You just let your tongue slide
Although when we talk
I may raise my voice
This is a heated conversation
So my tongue may be moist
And you may never want to stop
After you reach your destination
You never used to talk
But now you speak, with no hesitation
However, you must admit
This is good communication
Because we both get our point across
In an oral conversation

The Problem Is . . .

Like lotion
I'm soft on you
I want to rub this body
So soft on you
I want to escape
And get lost with you
I want this to be real
And not false with you
The problem is . . .

It's too soon to
Share flaws with you
I'm not sure if I should
Open some doors with you
Or hang a few pictures
On the walls with you
But I'm sure
I want to hit the stores
With you
That's no problem . . .

The question is . . .
Can we do some things together?
Like pray
And if I voice my opinion
Will you respect what I say?
Instead of putting your hands on me
Will you just walk away?

Why am I thinking about all of this today?
The problem is . . .
I just met you yesterday

A Movie

The show started
Let's make a movie
I want to watch you
Like a movie
The way you move me
Makes me woozy
I pour out like a waterfall
I'm a Jacuzzi
More like a river
Or a wave in the ocean
This wave in the ocean
Keeps me way in the ocean
What you do to me
It must be you and me
It's like it's new to me
I'm starring in a movie
You're in every chapter
Before and after
More than before
I want to know what's after
Give you an award
Because you're a hell of an actor
And since this is a movie
I want to give you an Oscar

Easy

I shed tears in the seat of my pants
Last night, Mr. Right and I danced
Slow wind, bump and grind
As the clock started ticking
We got lost in time

Yes, yes, he's mine
I'm thinking in my mind
When the clock stopped ticking
He came, running

To me, it meant I was in love
To him, it meant
I was just like any other woman
Easy

Slippery When Wet

Slippery when wet
Does this mean I'm falling in love?
Quick, quick somebody please catch me
I don't want to fall because I hate getting up

I feel like I'm losing my balance
I can't hold on, it's like I'm losing my grip
When it's slippery, how do I keep from falling?
When he's steady sinking my ship

I want to ride it, like a wave in the ocean
Part it like the red sea, and make you shiver
I want to slip and fall, but only in slow motion
I want to pour out my heart like a river

And if only for one night
I'll give you something you'll never forget
I slipped up and let you get me
It slipped in
Because it's so wet

Physical Attraction

He was standing there
I felt him breathing on me
Although it wasn't physical
I felt his hands all over me

Climbing my back like a ladder
Sending chills up and down my spine
Now this man never touched my body
But he reached in and touched my mind

Oh, what a feeling, to have him touch me
I close my eyes because it's like a dream
Physically, he never touched me
But he's already making me scream

As I stand there, hearing him breathe
I lean forward to get a reaction
Although this man never touched my body
It was physical, because it was satisfaction

My Daydream

You're awake
But you close your eyes and dream
In silence
Be still
I want to go off somewhere and scream

You're making me yearn for you
Shh, is this a dream?
I hear voices in the background
Someone's calling my name

Am awake but I feel like I am asleep
Excuse me, what's your name?
You keep repeating that
But I say nothing
I'm lost in my daydream

I just want to dream
In silence
Keep my dreams to myself
Because it's mine
My daydream

Peep Show

As I undress myself
Twirling, my hands in my braids
Someone's looking in my window
Pull down the shades

I'm in the mood to dance
So I turn my music on
Someone's looking in my window
Because I only have a tee shirt on

Although this dance is private
Someone's looking at me
But I'm not your private dancer
You're invading my privacy

So keep your windows closed
Because I'm putting my clothes back on
No more looking in my window
Your free peep show is gone

Men

What a creation God made
Although we don't understand them
Now, I love me some men
But at times, I can't stand them

It's strange
Because at times we don't connect
Our minds are in different places
And we didn't get to the same place yet

I would like to have more in common
Other than some real good sex
So what do we have in common?
Can we start with respect?

I love a passionate man
One who will treat me like a queen!
I will never settle for less
Because I'm a beautiful human being

Men
The opposite of me
Now I love me some men
But I need a real man
To handle me

Chapter Three:
In the Mind, There Was Pain and Healing

Protect Me, Lord

Sitting here pissed, mad at myself
I never had to wait for anything
But I'm sitting here waiting for results
I can't blame him
Because I opened that door
Because I knew he was celibate
I gave it to him raw
When he gave me the news
My heart dropped to the floor
Now I'm taking my heart
And putting it back in the draw
I need another chance
God, please, give me one more
You know me, Lord
I've never been through this before
I feel so ashamed
Because I'm the one who talks about it
I never thought, I'd be the one
Who has to sit and think about it
Lord, I don't want anything to come between us
Please hear my prayer
I don't even love sex that much
God, I know you're thinking
And I don't mean to interrupt
But if it means having my life
I'm willing to give it up
Did you hear what I said, God
I'm willing to give sex up
Because I love my life
And I'm not willing to give that up
Nothing means more to me
Than having good health
Now I'm asking you to protect me, Lord
Because I didn't protect myself

A Positive Person

You thought you were sure
Well it's confirmed, you're positive
And for the first time in your life
You wish you were negative

Be a positive person
You heard this all your life
But being positive today
Can change or end your life

Where did you go wrong?
Did they change the meaning of positive?
I guess being negative is a good thing
Especially when you're asking to live

So if you had a choice
Wouldn't you choose to live?
I'll be a positive person
If thinking positive
Means staying negative

She Kept Yelling Out

I'm not happy here
What's happening here?
Although the lights are on
It's pitch-black in here

Look in my eyes
Right between my eyes
And tell me, can you see
See through the cries

I got a pain
And I'm dealing with pain
And when I cry
It's like a puddle of rain

I want this pain out
Lord, take this pain out
Open up my heart
And let it drain out

I used to love me
I used to love you
But I don't love me
How can I love you?

This is my window
I see you looking through
No more lies
I want to tell the truth

No more rain
I want sunny skies
But how can I see?
With these black eyes

I can't close my eyes
I want to sleep at night
I know, if I pray
God will make it all right

I want to change me
I can't change you
I can only change me
I hope you change too

Even though you hit me
I kept coming back
A low self-esteem
Kept me coming back

But I'm tired of arguing
I'm tired of fighting
I got my pen and my pad
And I started writing

And this is why I'm writing
To help somebody out
I finally built up the nerve
To kick his ass out

B

Don't Call Him . . . Nigger

He took a lot of things
But don't call him nigger
He hated that word so much
He was willing to pull a trigger

He was angry, because all his life
He was judged by the color of his skin
But slavery was over years ago
And he's being called nigger again

Yeah, they called him nigger
And he was ready to explode
His gun loaded with bullets
And he was ready to unload

Keep walking, nigger, walk, nigger
That's what they kept on saying
As these visions came to his mind
Mr. Walker just kept on praying

But God was too slow with an answer
So Mr. Walker put his hand on the trigger
As he unloaded several shots
He yelled out
Don't call me nigger

Three Strikes Were Out

Strike One

We had fun in our bedroom
Especially when I wore my thong
But he only liked staying in the bedroom
Playing that same old song
Can we change the music?
The fun is starting to disappear
We used to have fun in the bedroom
You use to tickle your tongue in my ear

Strike Two

We're finally out of our bedroom
Don't understand it
But something's still missing
Although we're making love by the stove
We're no longer making love
Because we're no longer kissing
Can you whisper in my ear?
Oh, how I miss you sucking on my toes
I thought it would be better
To get out of the bedroom
But in the bedroom
You used to take off my clothes

Strike Three

She came into our bedroom
Now all three of us
Are in the bed naked
But it seemed
It was just the two of them
I watched his hands on her
And couldn't take it
Although we made it
Back in our bedroom
The mistake
Was bringing someone along
He stopped making love to me
But made love to her
All night long
Now I can't go back in our bedroom
It will always have me in doubt
We tried everything
To spice up our bedroom
But the answer was
For me to get out

Raped

He touched me, and I felt nothing
Just his sweat dripping on my face
He kept pounding
And wouldn't stop for nothing
Couldn't tell his sweat
From the tears in my face
I didn't yell or nothing
But I wanted to do something
But I didn't do anything
I guess I'm a disgrace
My innocence was ruined
Because of what he was doing
My precious jewels
Will never be replaced
I spent so many years
Buried under my tears
I've never been with a man
I couldn't face my fears
I pray that God forgives me
Because for so many years
I prayed for his death
Because I know who he is
Well, today he passed on
But my pain isn't gone
I'm still feeling the pain
Because I know, I prayed wrong
So, God, hear my prayer
Please forgive us for our sins
I pray, I can let this pain go
I pray that you let my father in

Rage

He kept to himself
Never said much
Never bothered anyone
He just got on the bus
But the bully in the class
Never let him pass
He hated everyone
Because he was being harassed
Angry inside
Because he didn't fit in
And he's building up rage
But he's holding it in

At home, they're yelling and screaming
"Fuck this, and I don't give a fuck about that
And boy, I'm tired of taking care of you
I hope you leave and never come back"

He grit his teeth
Because he's feeling the rage
He yells back, "I hope you rot in your grave"
He stole his father's money
And went and brought a gun
Now he's walking around campus
Looking to shoot someone
Pop, pop, pop
They heard shots in the parking lot
As the bully read the note by the bus

It said, "Today is your lucky day
I could've killed you
But if I kill myself
No one would make a fuss"

Blackout

I had a friend name Jill
She lived in a house, with a white picket fence
I always felt her parents were racist
I had a feeling but no evidence

They never spoke, they never smiled
I couldn't believe Jill invited me in her house
But guess what, they were never home
But they kept their lights on
Because they wanted us blacks out

Jill knew how her parents felt
But she didn't care because she wanted a friend
Although her parents always kept the blacks out
When they weren't home, she would let the blacks in

One day Jill's parents came home
And caught the neighborhood blacks in their house
That was the first time I saw a double barrel
They cocked it back and said
"All you niggers get out"

Something in Common

She thought she was in love
Because they had so much in common
Good food, good sex
And they both loved Common
They both loved to dress
Her hairdresser was Carmen
He undressed her with his eyes
For a guy, that was common
He made his way to her heart
And somehow got his charm in
Nice teeth, nice smile
And boy, is he charming
But the rage he would get in
Was somewhat alarming
He wouldn't let her in
But somehow, got a bomb in
As the clock started ticking
He was ready to explode
She didn't like what she was getting
So yes changed to no
But he held on too tight
And he wouldn't let go
She thought she was in love
Now she's six feet below
He heard voices in his mind
I guess the devil got in
He took his life too
Now, they have something in common

High, off life

I'm like a parachute in this world
I'm always reaching for the sky
It's like; I'm sitting on top of the world
Watching people down on earth get high
I'm high too, but in a different way
I get high off life
There's a difference between me and you
I'm living, and you're trying to get through life
Sometimes I'm up, sometimes I'm down
But I choose to be around those who loves me
But when you're up, you're really down
Because you chose to live a life, that's ugly
I'm high off life, and I'm having fun
I wouldn't give this drug up for the world
You're high off drugs
And you think you're having fun
Look around, there's nothing funny about your world
You can change the life you're living
All you have to do is give it a try
You can get high off life
You don't have to waste your life, getting high

Plain Clothes

Plain clothes doesn't get me noticed
I wear plaid skirts
And I don't get noticed
I dress like a lady
But always go un-noticed
I am a lady, did you notice?
You like short skirts
That's what I noticed
And, it's what's inside that count
But you wouldn't know this
The only thing you notice
Is my plain clothes

Nothing Like My Mother

My mother told me
I'll never amount to nothing
I look at my mother
And I see nothing
I feel nothing
Because she never felt nothing for me
But when I look in the mirror
I feel something for me

My mother told me
No one will ever love me
I knew my mother believed that
Because she felt nothing for me
When I look at my mother
All I see is something ugly

My mother never smiled
Never laughed
Never even gave me a hug
The one thing that I know
About my mother is,
My mother knows nothing
About love

I feel sorry for my mother
Because my mother's hiding under her pain
And I left all that pain with my mother
It's time for me to break that chain

My daughter was born today
She smiled at me, and what a beautiful girl
Today I know I'm nothing like my mother
Because my daughter
Is the greatest joy in my world

(Inspired by the motion picture Precious)

B

Home on the Train

We heard a beep, the doors opened up
People began rushing through the doors
I heard you speak, although I didn't understand you
Something like please don't scuff up my floors

Who invited all of you? I hate the weekdays
Because I get too many guests at one time
You guys never invite me to your homes
So please stop coming to mine

I looked up as if I agreed with you
All of a sudden you began to sing a note
You said, "Since nobody here is paying rent"
Leave some change so I can buy a new coat

No one answered your request
In fact everyone chose to ignore you
You were homeless and everyone could see
But it seemed like I was the only one who saw you

As the doors opened again
Everyone pushed and shoved
No one seemed to give a damn about you
Because everyone was in a rush

You said again, that's why you hate company
Because your floors get dirty when it rains
And most people have a home to go to
But your home is on the train

Affair

The time has arrived for us to go home
People were looking for us
Because we stayed out too long

You lived in a house, you never saw as home
Now no one's in your house
I guess you like when you're alone

I thought you did a lot for me
But all you did was make me moan
You never belonged to me
I just had you out on loan

I have my own house now
And it's time I start staying home
I have someone I don't have to share
And I like having my own

I'm leaving our affair behind me
You'll probably go back to doing your thing
You may be taking yours off now
But I'm ready to wear my ring

Ladies

He said he loved me
Over and over
But after we had sex
He gave me the cold shoulder
That bullshit love talk
Was finally over
He treated me like a dog
The way he had me bent over
Bitch, I want to hear you bark
So take this big bite
I let him treat me like a dog
Being misled by what's right
Ladies
Don't you know you're a jewel?
A man doesn't love you
If he treats you that cruel
You are beautiful, and yes
Do you know you're a gift?
And if a man doesn't respect you
He's not the one you should be with
So just look in the mirror
And you will see your beauty
You play a role in how he treats you
So start reporting to duty
And you don't have to settle
Wait for the man of your dreams
Ladies
Don't you know?
We are some beautiful queens

Someone's Crying for Help

A call from April

I want to ask for help
Because I'm finally ready to go
I wonder if I ask for help
Would you say yes?
Would you say no?
But before I ask for help
There's something that I must say
My name is April
And I am an alcoholic
I'm sober for the first time
In ten years today

A plea from Carol

Help somebody please
I just want to make it past the front door
I can't live my life in fear
I can't take these beatings anymore
I'm starting to hate men
I want to poison him when he eats
Would God forgive me more?
If I kill him in his sleep
Oh, Lord, if you're up there
This is a plea from Carol
Can you please answer my prayers?
Because I keep looking at this double barrel

Someone's crying for help
Should it matter who's making the call?
As long as there's help, when they're ready
Because we should be helping them all

B

Not in the Least

I didn't share the lease with her
But I thought at least, I mattered to her
Although this house never was my home
I saw myself at least with her

I ran her baths as the candles burned, slow
I was her chef, serving up the pot roast

My closet was the same as hers
Look in our closet
We wear the same clothes

She gave me keys
But never gave me a cent
Not on the lease, but I'm paying the rent
Baby at least, let's make this official
Split these bills so it won't be an issue

Call the landlord
Put my name on the lease
So at least, I can sleep in peace

I guess she never really wanted to do that
Because she removed all my shoes from the rack
I knew it was over
Because she took her keys back
And just like that, I was homeless

Locked

I stay locked in this house
The doors open
But I don't go outside
In this house
No one can see me
In this house
I can keep it inside
I can't remember the last time
I cut the lights on
It's dark in here
Because my light switch is gone
I can't remember the last time
I let some sun in
Sometimes I wish
I was never born
I can't remember the last time
I played some music
I can't remember the last time
I sang a song
In this house, I never play music
Because this house
Is another sad song
I stay locked in this house
And it was me
Who threw away the key
I can't remember the last time
I left this house
I don't come out
Because I'm locked inside of me

What's This World Coming To?

Questions I've asked in my mind
Makes me want to rhyme
We lost Michael Jackson
Let's remember the time
Press rewind, seek and find
Get in line
Let him shine
And let him
Rock with you
Until the end of time

So tell me
What's this world coming to?
A life lost
Right in front of you

Toasting his glass to his past
Ready to make it last
Heard a blast
With no badge
And bullets coming fast
Fifty shots from the cops
Packing gluts
You better watch
Sean Bell is dead
But yet we freed the cops

So tell me
What's this world coming to?
He got shot down
Right in front of you

No one can prove that he did it
I admit it
He put his hand in the glove
And couldn't fit it
Then got acquitted
But coma came back around
Just so he could get it
And even if he never admit it
He did it, he did it

So tell me
What's this world coming to?
He took two lives
Right in front of you

B

Cover Girl

She used to be very pretty
Now she's just a cover girl
Makeup all over her face
To hide the cuts and bruises
No one knows what she's going through
She doesn't come around anymore
Because the bruises are getting worse
Her eyes don't open wide anymore
I want to talk to her
Because I see the bloodstains in her pupils
So I decided to talk to her
She said, "Pain is something she's used to"
Then she told me that he loves her
And I just couldn't figure out why
I guess she needed someone to feel her pain
So her tears are coming out of my eyes
Although she puts on a lot of makeup
Her beauty will never be replaced
Now I know why
She's wearing all that makeup
She's covering up
All that pain on her face

These Eyes

Look into these eyes
And tell me what you see
With these eyes
I'm looking at you
And these eyes
See you looking at me

These eyes
Can identify your pain
I look at you
And see all I need to see

Tears in your eyes
Spells nothing but pain
I see it's you
Because I'm looking at me

What Is Poetry?

Poetry is love
Poetry can be pain
Poetry is deep
Like the blood in your vein
Poetry is like an intimate brain
Poetry is nature
Like the sun and rain
So what is poetry?

Poetry is the roses and the violets
We love to talk about
Poetry can be the violence
We don't like to speak about

Poetry is that verse in a song
That everyone wants to sing
But poetry speaks for itself
It has its own unique thing
So what is poetry?

Poetry can be a testimony
About something you've been through
And if you've got a story to tell
Then poetry is you

A Poem for God

God, you've done so much for me
I've asked you for direction
But you told me a story
Ever since I've praised you
You gave me the glory
So I'm giving it back to you
Because you wrote this story
You brought me out of darkness
Now I see the light
The only darkness I see now
Is when I pray to you at night
You're never too busy, God
And now I see
You are one of a kind
You are my Almighty God
And Almighty God
You stay on my mind
Keep giving me direction, Lord
Because at times, I may lose my way
Keep sending me the blessing, Lord
I pray for others every time I pray
When I walk through that valley, Lord
Please give me strength to carry on
Read that Holy Bible to me, Lord
You wrote my story
So I could write you this poem

CPSIA information can be obtained at www.ICGtesting.com
Printed in the USA
BVOW04s2254181113

336676BV00001B/100/P

9 781453 547939